MEET THE
LOS ANGELES LAKERS

BY LYLE SPENCER

SCHOLASTIC INC.

New York   Toronto   London   Auckland   Sydney
Mexico City   New Delhi   Hong Kong

PHOTO CREDITS:
NBA Entertainment Photos
Cover (O'Neal, Bryant), 24 (right, Smith), 11, 12 (Rider): Robert Mora. **Cover (Harper), 4, 5, 6, 8, 9, 12 (Fox), 15 (Celestand), 23 (Abdul-Jabbar), 24 (Rock, The Rock, Sandler, Carrey, Williamses), 26 (top left, bottom), 27 (bottom left, bottom right), 28 (top left, center), 29, 30, 31:** Andrew D. Bernstein. **7, 24 (Nicholson), 28 (bottom):** Garrett Ellwood. **10, 13 (Shaw), 28 (top right):** Sam Forencich. **13 (Fisher):** Jeff Reinking. **14 (George, Grant), 26 (top right):** Rocky Widner. **15 (Lue):** Bill Baptist. **18 (Jackson):** Barry Gossage. **18 (Winters, Hamblen, Cleamons):** Juan O'Campo. **18 (Bertka):** Jon Soohoo. **19:** Fernando Medina. **20 (Pollard), 22:** NBA Photo Library. **21 (Baylor):** Walter Iooss Jr. **21 (West):** Ken Regan. **27 (top):** Steve Woltmann.

20 (Mikan): Associated Press. **23 (Johnson), 25:** Sports Illustrated.

ISBN 0-439-24111-1

12 11 10 9 8 7 6 5 4 3 2 1   1 2 3 4 5/6

Printed in the U.S.A.
First Scholastic printing, February 2001
Book design: Michael Malone

MIKAN, WEST, ABDUL-JABBAR,

"SHOWTIME" STARRING MAGIC JOHNSON—

ALL CHAMPIONS. NOW, IN THE NEW

MILLENNIUM, THE LOS ANGELES LAKERS

HAVE BECOME THE FOCAL POINT OF THE

BASKETBALL WORLD ONCE AGAIN...

SUPERMAN—AND SUPERKID—TO THE RESCUE!

Led by their two super talents, Shaquille O'Neal and Kobe Bryant, the Los Angeles Lakers are once again the most exciting, most popular, and most talked-about team in the NBA. They pack their brand-new arena, STAPLES Center, with many of Hollywood's biggest stars and some of the NBA's most devoted fans, cheering their spectacular exploits.

Shaq, the Lakers' Superman, has stepped forward as the NBA's biggest, most powerful force. Shaq has even decorated his home and car with Man of Steel logos and memorabilia. Right by his side, faster than a speeding bullet, is Shaq's sensational young teammate, Kobe. In his fourth season, this 22-year-old guard has emerged as a true superstar, holding his own next to MVP Shaq.

For longtime Laker fans, Shaq and Kobe were the best thing to happen to the Lakers since the Showtime days of the 1980s. Then, Magic Johnson and Kareem Abdul-Jabbar ruled the NBA with five Lakers' championships and gave their fans more thrills than a season pass to Disneyland.

Shaq and Kobe were united in 1996. Shaq came to L.A. as a free agent from Orlando, and Kobe arrived as a 17-year-old rookie in a trade with the Charlotte Hornets. It took the pair a while to put everything together, but when they did, the rest of the NBA stood back, watching in amazement as the terrific twosome led their team to the team's first NBA Championship of the new millennium.

Guided by new coach Phil Jackson—leader of the six-time champion Chicago Bulls—Shaq, Kobe and their teammates have proven themselves to be the best team in the NBA. They won 67 games in 1999–2000 and lost only 15, even though Kobe missed the first 15 games with a broken right hand.

Their remarkable 1999–2000 season reminded fans of the glory days of the '80s, when the Lakers won those five championships. The Showtime Lakers won titles in 1980, 1982, 1985, 1987 and 1988. They were the first team to win back-to-back championships in 19 years.

Southern California waited patiently for the Lakers' return to glory. When it came, the fans had a season-long celebration. The new Lakers, led by Superman and Superkid, have truly brought Showtime back to the entertainment capital of the world.

Shaquille O'Neal wears a Man of Steel tattoo on his shoulder because of his favorite superhero, Superman. And, like Superman, this Man of Steel has taken flight with more power than a locomotive to become the NBA's most dominant and most valuable player.

The 7-1, 315-pound Shaq Diesel has always been a dominant and valuable player, but in 1999–2000, his fourth season in Los Angeles, he fit every phase of his game together perfectly.

In the 1999–2000 Most Valuable Player voting, Shaq received 120 of 121 first-place votes. Only one vote, for Philadelphia guard Allen Iverson, prevented Shaq from becoming the first player to ever be voted unanimously as MVP. Shaq also finished second to Miami's Alonzo Mourning in the Defensive Player of the Year voting.

In his eighth season in the NBA, 28-year-old Shaq finally fulfilled all the potential he showed throughout high school in San Antonio, at Louisiana State University, and during his first four NBA seasons with the Orlando Magic. Shaq led the NBA in scoring (29.7 points per game) and field goal percentage (.574). He was second in rebounding (13.6 per game) and third in blocked shots (3.03 per game), becoming the first player since legendary Laker Kareem Abdul-Jabbar in 1976–77 to finish in the top three in points, rebounds, blocks and field goal percentage. He also contributed more assists (3.8 per game) than in any other season in his career.

Already larger than life as an actor—in *Blue Chips* and *Kazaam*, a rapper and endorsement personality, and boasting a gold medal from the 1996 Summer Games in Atlanta, Shaq has finally arrived at the top of his profession: He is the NBA's best player.

CAREER HIGHLIGHTS
- Schick NBA Rookie of the Year: 1993
- NBA scoring champion: 1995, 2000
- NBA All-Star: 1993–98, 2000
- Olympic gold medalist: 1996
- NBA Most Valuable Player: 2000

DID YOU KNOW? *Shaq scored a career-high 61 points against the Los Angeles Clippers at the STAPLES Center on his 28th birthday, March 6, 2000.*

SHAQUILLE O'NEAL	NO. 34				YEARS IN THE NBA: 8		

POSITION	HEIGHT/WEIGHT		BIRTH DATE		COLLEGE		
Center	7-1/315		3/6/72		Louisiana State		

	GP	FG%	FT%	RPG	APG	PPG	PTS
1999–2000:	79	.574	.524	13.6	3.8	29.7	2,344
Career:	534	.577	.534	12.4	2.7	27.5	14,687

Superstar

No longer does anyone worry about Kobe Bryant's age—he's 22—or his lack of experience. He has put all concerns to rest by becoming one of the NBA's greatest all-around players.

The only question now is whether Kobe is better offensively or defensively. Because of a broken bone in his hand, Kobe had to miss the first 15 games of the 1999–2000 season, then had to make a difficult adjustment to the Lakers' new Triangle offense. But Kobe immediately showed that he was ready to lead his team, and 1999–2000 proved to be a spectacular season. The Lakers lost only one of the first 21 games Kobe played after returning to his guard position.

The Lakers had been waiting for Kobe to become a confident, patient player, and everything finally came together in his fourth season. He averaged 22.5 points per game, while leading the team in assists and steals, and finished second to Shaq in rebounds.

He was named to the NBA All-Defensive First Team for the first time, a remarkable achievement considering that Michael Jordan didn't do that until he was 25. Kobe is able to defend small guards, big guards and small forwards. He can take over for anyone the coaches need to cool down.

The son of former NBA player Joe "Jelly Bean" Bryant, Kobe came to the Lakers in 1996 in a trade with Charlotte. The Hornets, who took Kobe, a 17-year-old senior from Lower Merion High in Ardmore, Pennsylvania, in the first round, acquired Vlade Divac from the Lakers in the deal. Lakers fans have been thanking Vlade and the Hornets for giving them Kobe ever since.

CAREER HIGHLIGHTS

- *USA Today* High School Player of the Year after leading Lower Merion to Pennsylvania Class AAAA state championship: 1996
- All-Star Slam-Dunk champion: 1997
- Youngest player ever to start an NBA All-Star Game: 1998
- Two-time All-Star Game starter: 1998, 2000
- NBA All-Defensive First Team: 1999–2000
- All-NBA Second Team: 1999–2000

DID YOU KNOW? *Kobe lived in Italy as a child and loved to study tapes sent by friends of his favorite NBA player: the Lakers' Magic Johnson. Now Kobe keeps a part of his Italian childhood with him as an NBA player: He owns 50 percent of Olimpia Milano, a team in the Italian professional league.*

KOBE BRYANT		NO. 8			YEARS IN THE NBA: 4		
POSITION	**HEIGHT/WEIGHT**		**BIRTH DATE**		**HIGH SCHOOL**		
Guard	6-7/210		8/23/78		Lower Merion, PA		
	GP	**FG%**	**FT%**	**RPG**	**APG**	**PPG**	**PTS**
1999–2000:	66	.468	.821	6.3	4.9	22.5	1,485
Career:	266	.450	.816	4.0	3.0	15.9	4,240

Floor Leader

When the Lakers signed Ron Harper, there was no doubt about his job description. He was going to be Phil Jackson's coach on the floor, teaching the team how to run the complicated triangle offense Harper had helped Michael Jordan and Scottie Pippen run during his five years in Chicago.

Harper quickly assumed the role of team leader, team jokester and unofficial spokesman. He started all but four games in 1999–2000, his 14th season, and his experience proved instrumental to the Lakers' success. Jackson looked to Ron to call signals at both ends of the court and play solid defense. Early in his career, Ron was known as a scorer. He averaged 22.9 points as a rookie for Cleveland in 1986–87 and averaged between 18.0 and 22.8 in four-plus seasons with the Clippers. But a serious knee injury—and age—forced him to change into a fabulous defensive stopper and a passer, rather than a leading scorer.

RON HARPER			NO. 4		YEARS IN THE NBA: 14		

POSITION	HEIGHT/WEIGHT		BIRTH DATE		COLLEGE		
Guard	6-6/216		1/20/64		Miami of Ohio		

	GP	FG%	FT%	RPG	APG	PPG	PTS
1999–2000:	80	.399	.680	4.2	3.4	7.0	557
Career:	962	.445	.720	4.3	4.0	14.1	13,603

DID YOU KNOW? *When he came into the NBA in 1986, Ron was compared to Michael Jordan because of his great leaping ability and skills. Little did Ron know that he and Michael would end up being teammates in Chicago years later and would win three championships together.*

CAREER HIGHLIGHTS

- Second-Team All-America at Miami (Ohio): 1986
- NBA All-Rookie Team: 1987
- Led Clippers into playoffs: 1992, 1993
- Three-time NBA champion in Chicago: 1996, 1997, 1998

ROBERT HORRY

Robert Horry is the kind of player every championship team needs: unselfish, versatile, cool under fire and always at his best when it counts the most. Acquired from Phoenix in 1997, Robert has become the same dynamic force he was in Houston, when he helped Hakeem Olajuwon and the Rockets win back-to-back championships in 1994 and '95. In the '95 Finals, as the Rockets swept Shaq and Orlando in four straight, Robert averaged 17.8 points.

Robert comes off the bench at power forward, bringing great energy and athletic ability. Defensively, his long arms and anticipation make him a threat to steal the ball and race the other way. He is also one of the fastest players in the league and an excellent rebounder. Offensively, Robert can score from anywhere on the court. His three-point baskets have brought the Lakers back many times and help to fire up the home crowd.

Clutch Performer

ROBERT HORRY	NO. 5			YEARS IN THE NBA: 8			
POSITION	**HEIGHT/WEIGHT**		**BIRTH DATE**	**COLLEGE**			
Forward	6-10/235		8/25/70	Alabama			
	GP	FG%	FT%	RPG	APG	PPG	PTS
1999–2000:	76	.438	.788	4.8	1.6	5.7	436
Career:	535	.449	.732	5.3	2.6	8.8	4,692

CAREER HIGHLIGHTS
- First-Team All-Southeastern Conference: 1990
- NBA All-Rookie Second Team: 1993
- Won NBA titles with Houston Rockets: 1994, 1995
- Set NBA Finals record for steals in a game (7): 1995

DID YOU KNOW? *Robert made the difficult transition from small forward, where his athletic skills were more naturally suited, to power forward as a Laker. He was able to more than hold his own, even though he was getting roughed up regularly by heavier players.*

RICK FOX 17

A smart, versatile veteran with the strength and athletic ability to defend small or power forwards, Rick Fox is a pivotal member of the Lakers' second unit after being a starter for most of his career in Boston and Los Angeles. He did not miss a regular-season game in 1999–2000, bringing nonstop hustle, energy, a dangerous outside shot and a relentless attitude on the boards to every game.

RICK FOX		NO. 17				YEARS IN THE NBA: 9	
POSITION	**HEIGHT/WEIGHT**		**BIRTH DATE**		**COLLEGE**		
Forward	6-7/242		7/24/69		North Carolina		
	GP	FG%	FT%	RPG	APG	PPG	PTS
1999–2000:	82	.414	.808	2.4	1.7	6.5	534
Career:	652	.459	.768	3.6	2.7	10.2	6,670

ISAIAH RIDER 7

An explosive scorer, Isaiah Rider joins the Lakers after one year in Atlanta. Isaiah scored flurries of points in Minnesota and Portland before moving to Atlanta for the 1999–2000 season. Isaiah will finally get the opportunity of a lifetime, now that he has signed as a free agent with the team he admired as a kid growing up in Northern California.

ISAIAH RIDER		NO. 7				YEARS IN THE NBA: 7	
POSITION	**HEIGHT/WEIGHT**		**BIRTH DATE**		**COLLEGE**		
Guard	6-5/215		3/12/71		Nevada-Las Vegas		
	GP	FG%	FT%	RPG	APG	PPG	PTS
1999–2000:	60	.419	.785	4.3	3.7	19.3	1,158
Career:	486	.444	.811	4.1	2.9	18.1	8,805

DEREK FISHER 2

A fan favorite for his hustling, team-first attitude, in 1999–2000 Derek Fisher gave up his starting position to veteran Ron Harper without complaint and continued to play with great heart and energy off the bench. Derek improved his scoring average from 5.9 to 6.3 points per game while playing solid defense.

DEREK FISHER		NO. 2			YEARS IN THE NBA: 4		
POSITION	**HEIGHT/WEIGHT**		**BIRTH DATE**		**COLLEGE**		
Guard	6-1/200		8/9/74		Arkansas-Little-Rock		
	GP	**FG%**	**FT%**	**RPG**	**APG**	**PPG**	**PTS**
1999–2000:	78	.346	.724	1.8	2.8	6.3	491
Career:	290	.385	.724	1.8	3.0	5.4	1,570

BRIAN SHAW 20

Playing for his seventh NBA team in 11 seasons, Brian Shaw has emerged as a valued backcourt reserve, giving the Lakers smart decision-making, inspired defense and clutch shooting. He is especially adept at throwing the lob pass to Shaq, his former Orlando team-mate. Brian began his career as a starter in Boston but is happy to be back home in California, doing whatever is necessary to make the Lakers a winner.

BRIAN SHAW		NO. 20			YEARS IN THE NBA: 11		
POSITION	**HEIGHT/WEIGHT**		**BIRTH DATE**		**COLLEGE**		
Guard	6-6/200		3/22/66		UC-Santa Barbara		
	GP	**FG%**	**FT%**	**RPG**	**APG**	**PPG**	**PTS**
1999–2000:	74	.382	.759	2.9	2.7	4.1	305
Career:	733	.406	.785	3.6	4.7	7.8	5,707

DEVEAN GEORGE 3

Devean George was the Lakers' 1999 first-round draft pick from Augsburg College, a small school in Minnesota. Devean has already shown flashes of great things to come in his limited duty off the bench. His three-point shooting and wide range of athletic skills remind some experts of a young Scottie Pippen. Devean has great potential and could become a familiar name to Lakers fans for years to come.

DEVEAN GEORGE		NO. 3			YEARS IN THE NBA: 1		
POSITION	**HEIGHT/WEIGHT**		**BIRTH DATE**		**COLLEGE**		
Forward	6-8/220		8/29/77		Augsburg (Minn.)		
	GP	FG%	FT%	RPG	APG	PPG	PTS
1999–2000:	49	.389	.659	1.5	0.2	3.2	155

HORACE GRANT 54

Acquired in a blockbuster trade during the off-season, Horace Grant fits the Lakers like a glove. Horace, a 6-10, 245-pound power forward, is the perfect complement to center Shaquille O'Neal, and adds much-needed muscle to the Lakers' frontline. This is a reunion of sorts for Horace and Shaq, who were teammates for two seasons in Orlando and together helped lead the Magic to the 1995 NBA Finals. The Lakers are hoping their chemistry is just as magical in Los Angeles.

HORACE GRANT		NO. 54			YEARS IN THE NBA: 13		
POSITION	**HEIGHT/WEIGHT**		**BIRTH DATE**		**COLLEGE**		
Forward	6-10/245		7/4/65		Clemson		
	GP	FG%	FT%	RPG	APG	PPG	PTS
1999–2000:	76	.444	.721	7.8	2.5	8.1	612
Career:	952	.513	.686	8.6	2.4	12.1	11,482

TYRONN LUE 10

A super-quick guard with exceptional potential, Tyronn Lue suffered an injured right knee and was forced to undergo surgery in November 1999, limiting him to only eight games in his second NBA season. As a rookie out of Nebraska in 1998, Tyronn became a crowd favorite with his all-out hustle and knack for hitting three-point shots.

TYRONN LUE	NO. 10				YEARS IN THE NBA: 2		
POSITION	**HEIGHT/WEIGHT**		**BIRTH DATE**		**COLLEGE**		
Guard	6-0/175		5/3/77		Nebraska		
	GP	FG%	FT%	RPG	APG	PPG	PTS
1999–2000:	8	.487	.750	1.5	2.1	6.0	48
Career:	23	.452	.621	0.8	1.8	5.3	123

JOHN CELESTAND 11

A point guard from Villanova, John Celestand impressed the Lakers with his defense and attitude, but his rookie year was limited to only 16 games because of tendinitis in his left knee. But John showed enough talent in those rare appearances to impress Phil Jackson, who indicated at the end of the 1999–2000 season that Celestand will get a good shot at extended playing time in 2000–2001.

JOHN CELSTAND	NO. 11				YEARS IN THE NBA: 1		
POSITION	**HEIGHT/WEIGHT**		**BIRTH DATE**		**COLLEGE**		
Guard	6-4/178		3/6/77		Villanova		
	GP	FG%	FT%	RPG	APG	PPG	PTS
1999–2000:	16	.333	.833	0.7	1.3	2.3	37

COREY HIGHTOWER

Taken in the second round by San Antonio and acquired by the Lakers in a trade, Corey Hightower, the 6-8, 200-pound guard from Indian Hills Community College (Ottumwa, Iowa), who grew up in Flint, Michigan, impressed the coaching staff with his deft shooting touch and athleticism. He'll be brought into the lineup gradually, as a potential swingman.

MARK MADSEN

Energetic, hard-nosed, and an academic All-America, Mark Madsen drew comparisons to former Laker Kurt Rambis when he was taken in the first round of the NBA Draft out of Stanford, where he finished his career as the sixth-best rebounder in school history. Mark, a 6-9, 240-pound power forward, led the Pacific-10 Conference in field goal percentage (.587) as a senior and was a driving force in the Cardinal's journey to the Final Four as a sophomore, averaging 15.2 points and 12.2 rebounds in the NCAA Tournament.

STANISLAV MEDVEDENKO

A versatile 6-10 forward who has been a member of the Ukraine National Team since 1998, Stanislav Medvedenko, 21, was signed as a free agent after leading BC Kiev to the Northern European Basketball League championship, averaging 20 points and 6.1 rebounds. He's the first European-born player to sign with the Lakers since Vlade Divac in 1989.

So you think you know the Lakers?

1. **Which Laker assistant coach played for the Lakers' 1971-72 championship team?**
   A) Bill Bertka   B) Jim Cleamons   C) Frank Hamblen

2. **Where did Shaquille O'Neal go to college?**
   A) North Carolina   B) Texas   C) Louisiana State

3. **Which former NBA coach was Phil Jackson's college coach at North Dakota?**
   A) Bill Fitch   B) Jack Ramsay   C) Dick Motta

4. **Which Laker was Shaq's teammate in Orlando and also a teammate of Larry Bird in Boston?**
   A) John Salley   B) Ron Harper   C) Brian Shaw

5. **Which Laker is married to the actress/singer Vanessa Williams?**
   A) Brian Shaw   B) Robert Horry   C) Rick Fox

6. **Which Laker made it to the playoffs for two seasons as a Los Angeles Clipper?**
   A) Ron Harper   B) A.C. Green   C) John Salley

7. **Which team did head coach Phil Jackson win a championship with as a player?**
   A) Chicago Bulls   B) Boston Celtics   C) New York Knicks

8. **Which Laker is named after a type of steak?**
   A) Shaquille O'Neal   B) Mark Madsen   C) Kobe Bryant

9. **Which Laker was a member of the 1995 NBA Champion Houston Rockets?**
   A) Brian Shaw   B) Robert Horry   C) Derek Fisher

10. **Which Laker grew up in Italy and speaks fluent Italian?**
    A) Derek Fisher   B) Kobe Bryant   C) Travis Knight

Answers: 1.C, 2.C, 3.C, 4.A, 5.C, 6.A, 7.C, 8.C, 9.B, 10.B

COACHES
INSPIRATION, MOTIVATION, IMAGINATION

Phil Jackson

Tex Winters

Bill Bertka

Frank Hamblen

Jim Cleamons

When the Lakers signed Phil Jackson as their coach in the summer of 1999, Vice Presidents Jerry West and Magic Johnson and General Manager Mitch Kupchak all agreed that they had hired the best coach in the business.

Jackson's record with the Chicago Bulls showed his ability to inspire, motivate and direct teams. The Lakers' executives were hoping he could do the same with their team.

Jackson won six championships with the Bulls, in 1991, 1992, 1993, 1996, 1997 and 1998. He did it by stressing team play with Michael Jordan, Scottie Pippen and their teammates. Jackson has always considered teamwork the most important aspect of any team, which goes back to his playing days in New York with the Knicks. He saw that the Knicks could beat teams with superior individual talent by playing together with intelligence and poise.

Jackson was coached in New York by the legendary Red Holzman, who won two NBA titles(1970 and '73). Holzman's Knicks were famous for their great teamwork and defense, qualities that would later become Jackson's trademarks in Chicago and now in Los Angeles.

Jackson brought with him to the West Coast three of his assistants from Chicago: Tex Winters, Jim Cleamons and Frank Hamblen. They were joined by Bill Bertka, who has been with the Lakers' organization for many years and worked as Pat Riley's chief aide during the team's Showtime era of the 1980s.

Winters has been coaching at the college and pro levels for a half century. It is his offensive strategy, known as the Triangle, that the Lakers used to create improved passing and movement while helping free up more room for Shaquille O'Neal to operate.

The biggest improvement in the Lakers' play has been at the defensive end of the court. Shaq and Kobe Bryant are the key figures—both were voted among the league's top five defenders —but others, including the ready reserves, play key roles.

"Defense is the cornerstone of our team," Kobe has said. "We've become much more focused on defense this season than we were in the past."

Jackson's 67-15 record with the Lakers in 1999–2000 was the second best in NBA history for a first-year coach. Only Bill Sharman's with the 1971–72 Lakers, who were 69-13, was better.

"This team came together much faster than I had expected," Jackson said. "It's a tribute to the players and their willingness to work and improve. It wasn't easy learning a whole new system, but they did a great job."

Jackson's career record of 612–208, for a 74.6% winning percentage, is the best in NBA history. His next statistical target is nine coaching titles, the record held by Boston's Red Auerbach. He only has two to go.

DYNAMIC DUOS

SHAQUILLE
O'NEAL

KOBE BRYANT

It's no secret that Shaquille O'Neal got all A's this year from his strict teacher, Phil Jackson. Shaq is diligent about his homework. One of his favorite subjects is NBA history. And he plans to make a lot of it with Kobe Bryant and their Laker teammates.

"As a student of the game," Shaq says, "I realize every great team has a one-two punch. Our one-two punch is me and Kobe. Phil is the type of coach who lets us take advantage of the matchups we get."

Throughout NBA history, starting with the Minneapolis Lakers in the late 1940s, the best teams have had two big stars, surrounded by role players willing to sacrifice the spotlight for the team's benefit.

Basketball's first great big man was a Laker, and his name was George Mikan. The man from DePaul wore glasses and, at 6-10, towered over his rivals, leading the league in scoring six times and averaging 22.6 points in his career. He was the Shaq of his era, the league's first superstar, when the Lakers still played in Minneapolis.

The Kobe of that great Lakers team that won five championships in six years from 1949 through 1954 ('49, '50, '52, '53, '54) was Jim Pollard. The Stanford graduate stood 6-5, just about Kobe's height, and was the first great leaper in basketball. Known as the "Kangaroo Kid," Pollard did reverse dunks long before they became commonplace and played in a slashing style very similar to Kobe's. The dynamic duo of Mikan and Pollard led the Minneapolis Lakers to NBA dominance throughout the early '50s.

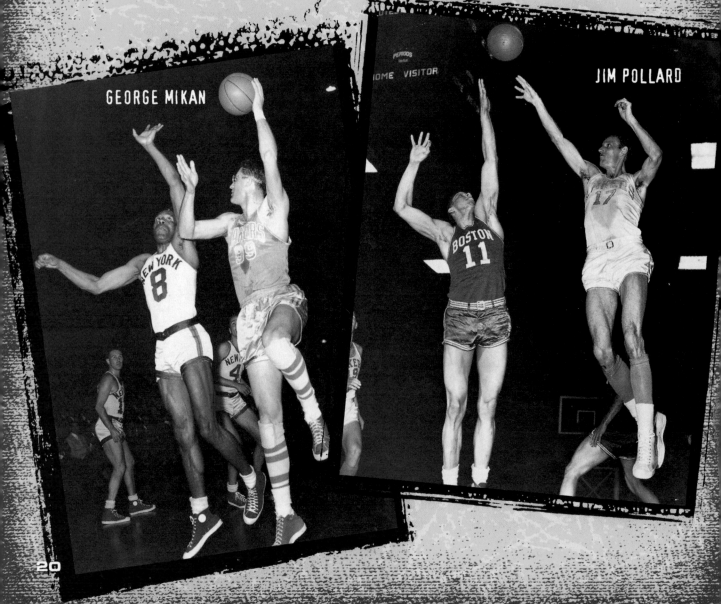

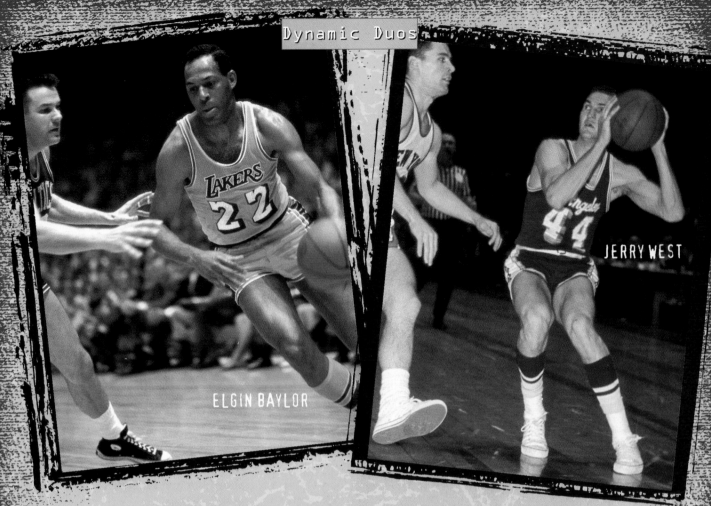

ELGIN BAYLOR

JERRY WEST

Even though the Boston Celtics, with legendary great Bill Russell, dominated the next era, the Lakers had the league's best one-two punch to challenge the Celtics. Elgin Baylor and Jerry West, playing in the new Laker home, Los Angeles, thrilled crowds with their spectacular scoring feats.

Baylor, a 6-5 forward with amazing rebounding ability, and West, a 6-2 guard who was a great defender as well as the Mr. Clutch of NBA scorers, led the Lakers into six NBA Finals against Boston. They came close each time but were always frustrated by Russell and the Celtics.

Baylor, 11 times an All-Star, and West, a 14-time All-Star, are the third and fifth best scorers in league history. Baylor averaged 27.4 points per game, West 27.0. The only players ahead of them are Michael Jordan, Wilt Chamberlain and Shaquille O'Neal who, at #4, is behind Baylor.

Baylor retired in 1971, and the Lakers ironically went on to win their first title in Los Angeles that season. The Lakers' new dynamic duo featured West with the great Big Dipper, Wilt Chamberlain.

Chamberlain was the most dominant center in league history, a 7-1 giant who controlled the boards, blocked shots and scored in record numbers. He even shot a record 100 points in one game. Upon arriving in L.A., he sacrificed his scoring to pass, rebound and block shots. It was his defense, combined with the offense of

West and Gail Goodrich, that powered the Lakers to a 33-game winning streak and the 1971–72 NBA championship.

The Lakers' next great pair debuted in 1979, when Earvin "Magic" Johnson arrived from the Michigan State campus, having led the Spartans to the NCAA title. It was instant magic between the charismatic 6-9 point guard and the Lakers' current 7-2 superstar center, Kareem Abdul-Jabbar, who had won three NCAA titles at UCLA and one NBA crown as a Milwaukee Buck in 1971.

Magic and Kareem quickly became the most productive duo in league history, driving the Lakers to five championships and eight trips to the Finals in the 1980s. The magic began in Johnson's rookie season, when he took over in the NBA Finals when Kareem was sidelined by an ankle injury. Magic scored 42 points with 15 rebounds and seven assists in the decisive Game 6 of the Finals at Philadelphia.

Showtime had arrived, in all its spectacular glory, and Kareem became the Lakers' and NBA's all-time scoring champion. Magic and Kareem, surrounded by such exceptional teammates as Norm Nixon, Jamaal Wilkes, James Worthy, Michael Cooper, Byron Scott, Bob McAdoo, Kurt Rambis and Mitch Kupchak, drove the Lakers to championships in '80, '82, '85, '87 and '88. The '85 title probably meant the most to them—it was won

WILT CHAMBERLAIN

MAGIC JOHNSON

KAREEM ABDUL-JABBAR

in Boston Garden, where Lakers teams had experienced so much heartbreak during the '60s.

After Kareem retired in 1989, Magic made it to the Finals one last time, in '91, but his team was beaten by Jordan and the Bulls.

In the summer of '96, the Lakers traded with Charlotte for rights to Kobe Bryant, a 17-year-old coming out of Lower Merion High School in Ardmore, Pennsylvania, and then signed Shaquille O'Neal as a free agent.

Kobe and Shaq had some growing pains together for three seasons, but it all came together in 1999–2000. Shaq became the league's Most Valuable Player with his best season, leading the league in scoring and field goal accuracy while finishing second in rebounding and third in blocked shots. Kobe was all-league first-team defense and the Lakers' second-best scorer, raising his game to such a level that experts have begun comparing him to Michael Jordan. Kobe and Shaq have become the Lakers' new pair for the new millennium.

From Mikan and Pollard, to Baylor and West, to West and Chamberlain, to Magic and Kareem, to Kobe and Shaq . . . no team in sports has ever had so many truly dynamic duos.

Home, Sweet Home

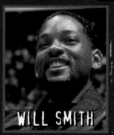

CHRIS ROCK

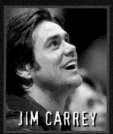

JACK NICHOLSON

THE ROCK

WILL SMITH

ADAM SANDLER

JIM CARREY

VENUS & SERENA WILLIAMS

In addition to welcoming a new coaching staff and four new players, the 1999-2000 Lakers moved into a dazzling new home, **STAPLES** Center, in downtown Los Angeles. After 33 years at the Great Western Forum in Inglewood, where they won six championships and thrilled fans with some of the greatest players and performances in basketball history, the team moved about 15 miles away, into the heart of the city.

With a seating capacity of 19,282 for Lakers' games, **STAPLES** Center became the meeting place for many of Hollywood's biggest stars. The great Bruce Springsteen opened the arena, and it kept on rocking as the home of the Los Angeles Clippers and the Los Angeles Kings (National Hockey League), as well as the home of the Lakers.

The closing of the Forum, which was home to Hall of Famers Elgin Baylor, Jerry West, Wilt Chamberlain, Gail Goodrich, Kareem Abdul-Jabbar and Magic Johnson, was the end of a wonderful era.

"What memories, from Elgin and Jerry all the way to Shaq and Kobe!" recalled Chick Hearn, who is the Hall of Fame play-by-play voice of the Lakers. "But now it's on to a new building, a new era. It's exciting, baby!" The popular Chickie Baby has broadcast more than 3,200 consecutive games (and counting!), bringing his exciting word's-eye view to millions of fans, and has moved with the Lakers into a new era and a new arena.

A Magic Moment

The Lakers' return to the NBA Finals in 2000 came on the 20th anniversary of one of the most amazing chapters in Lakers' team history.

There was magic in the air in Philadelphia for Game 6 of the 1980 Finals. The Lakers were leading the powerful 76ers three games to two, but their dominating center, Kareem Abdul-Jabbar, had injured his ankle near the end of Game 5 and did not join the team for the flight to Philadelphia.

All the experts assumed the 76ers would win easily and force a Game 7 back in Los Angeles. But it was doubtful the great Kareem would have been ready to play. The injury was considered serious, and he was unable to walk when the team left home for Philadelphia.

Shorthanded without their big man, the Lakers turned to 20-year-old rookie Earvin "Magic" Johnson for leadership, as well as scoring, rebounding, passing and defense.

MAGIC JOHNSON

Magic, who one year earlier had led Michigan State to the NCAA championship, responded with one of the greatest performances in NBA history. He came into the game a mere rookie, and left a hero and a star.

By the time the game was over, the Philadelphia fans were silent. The only celebrating being done in Philly was by the 11 Lakers and their coaching staff. They had won their first title in eight seasons, thanks to Magic's 42 points, 15 rebounds and seven assists.

"It was a dream game, the greatest of my life," said Magic, who now is the Lakers' part-owner and vice president. "Nobody gave us a chance. Everyone in Philly just knew they were gonna kill us. But I told the guys, 'Have no fear. They won't be able to keep up with us. We'll run, run, run, just keep running 'em.'"

The bigger, stronger 76ers could not keep up with the swifter Lakers, just as Magic had predicted in a pregame talk with his teammates. Jamaal Wilkes, a slender Laker forward, also had one of his greatest games, with 37 points.

That game was the start of a decade-long dynasty for the Lakers. They won championships again in 1982, 1985, 1987 and 1988, and made it to the Finals before losing in 1983, 1984 and 1989.

The leader of Showtime, and the most charismatic player of his time was Earvin "Magic" Johnson, who always remembers that magical day in Philadelphia as his greatest ever. It was the day he truly arrived as an NBA superstar.

THE YEAR IN PICTURES

RESPECT YOUR ELDERS. RON HARPER USES HIS VETERAN SKILLS TO SLIDE PAST THE YOUNGER SACRAMENTO KINGS' POINT GUARD, JASON WILLIAMS.

KOBE BRYANT SHOWS THAT WORKING TO WIN A CHAMPIONSHIP DOESN'T MEAN YOU CAN'T HAVE FUN ALONG THE WAY.

PROFESSOR PHIL JACKSON GIVES HIS EAGER PUPILS A LESSON ON THE FINER POINTS OF BASKETBALL.

ELEVATOR GOING UP. RICK FOX GOES AIRBORNE AGAINST THE ORLANDO MAGIC'S JOHN AMAECHI TO CONVERT A LAYUP.

SUPERMAN TO THE RESCUE! SHAQUILLE O'NEAL GETS READY TO CRUISE DOWN THE STREETS OF L.A.

SHOOTING FOR THE STARS. BRIAN SHAW SHAKES OFF HIS DEFENDER AND POPS THE OPEN JUMPER.

LAKERS RETIRED NUMBERS

13
WILT CHAMBERLAIN

The most dominating player of his time, the 7-1 "Big Dipper" set records that will probably never be broken. He scored 100 points in a game in 1962 when he played for the Philadelphia Warriors and averaged 50.4 points per game for the season. He led two different teams to championships during his 14-year career.

22
ELGIN BAYLOR

The first truly spectacular player in NBA history, Baylor made soaring moves to the hoop that have been copied by many of the greats who came after him, such as Julius Erving and Michael Jordan. Elgin averaged 27.4 points per game in 14 seasons and was a first-team all-league forward 10 times.

25
GAIL GOODRICH

Affectionately called "Stumpy" by his teammates because of his average size, Goodrich had an amazing knack for creating shots and making them. He joined Jerry West in one of the best backcourts in NBA history for the 1971–72 championship Lakers.

32
MAGIC JOHNSON

The leader of the Showtime Lakers, Magic never cared about personal statistics. A three-time NBA MVP, he was the man who made all his teammates better, playing a total team game while driving his teams to five championships in the 1980s. A first-team all-NBA player nine times, he crowned his career by leading the 1992 U.S. Dream Team to an Olympic gold medal in Barcelona.

LAKERS RETIRED NUMBERS

33
KAREEM ABDUL-JABBAR

With an unequaled combination of power and grace, Kareem established the all-time NBA scoring record, using as his foremost weapon the unstoppable sky-hook. Kareem was a league MVP a record six times and played on six championship teams, five with the Lakers and one with Milwaukee. He was first-team all-NBA 10 times. The Bucks sent the former UCLA great to the Lakers in 1975 in one of the biggest trades in NBA history.

42
JAMES WORTHY

"Big Game James" he was called, for his amazing ability to play at his highest level when the pressure was turned up the most. Worthy came to the Lakers from North Carolina, where he played with Michael Jordan and led the Tar Heels to the 1982 NCAA title. An unstoppable force, James played for three NBA championship teams and was the MVP of the 1988 Finals against Detroit.

44
JERRY WEST

"Mr. Clutch" was the greatest pressure player of his time, making an incredible number of game-winning and game-tying shots in the last seconds with one of the prettiest jump shots in history. Ten times a first-team all-NBA guard, Jerry also was a fabulous defensive player. He became the NBA's most successful executive after his playing days, building the Showtime Lakers and making the moves in 1996 that brought Shaquille O'Neal and Kobe Bryant to Los Angeles.

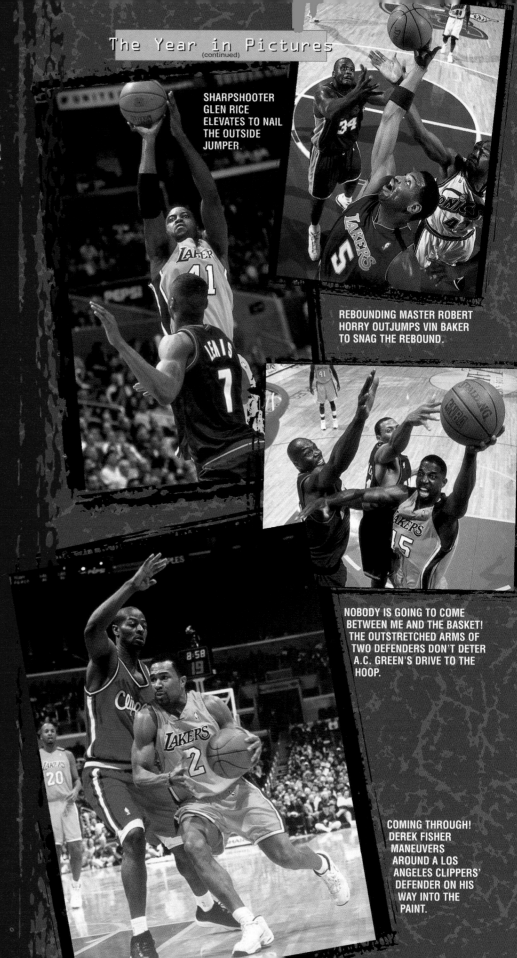

SHARPSHOOTER GLEN RICE ELEVATES TO NAIL THE OUTSIDE JUMPER.

REBOUNDING MASTER ROBERT HORRY OUTJUMPS VIN BAKER TO SNAG THE REBOUND.

NOBODY IS GOING TO COME BETWEEN ME AND THE BASKET! THE OUTSTRETCHED ARMS OF TWO DEFENDERS DON'T DETER A.C. GREEN'S DRIVE TO THE HOOP.

COMING THROUGH! DEREK FISHER MANEUVERS AROUND A LOS ANGELES CLIPPERS' DEFENDER ON HIS WAY INTO THE PAINT.

PLAYOFFS
ROUND 1

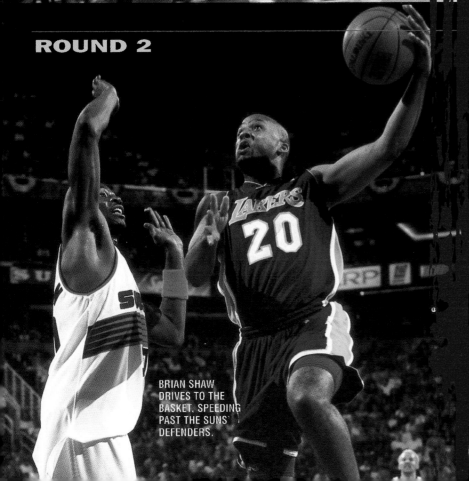

JOHN SALLEY LOOKS FOR
AN OPENING DURING A GAME
AGAINST THE KINGS.

ROUND 2

BRIAN SHAW
DRIVES TO THE
BASKET, SPEEDING
PAST THE SUNS'
DEFENDERS.

THE REAL KINGS

When Shaquille O'Neal powered to 46 points in Game 1 and Kobe Bryant soared to 32 points to lead a Game 2 victory, the Lakers looked unstoppable against Sacramento. But the Kings, led by power forward Chris Webber and ex-Laker Vlade Divac, came through for their home fans in Games 3 and 4. They won both games, despite 35 points by Kobe in Game 3 and 32 by Kobe in Game 4. With the season on the line in Game 5, the Lakers responded with an overpowering performance to move on to Round 2.

GAME 1
LAKERS 117, Kings 107

GAME 2
LAKERS 113, Kings 89

GAME 3
KINGS 99, Lakers 91

GAME 4
KINGS 101, Lakers 88

GAME 5
LAKERS 113, Kings 86

BLOCKING OUT THE SUNS

Once again, it was the Shaq and Kobe Show in the Western Conference semifinals. Shaq came out with 37 points in Game 1 against Phoenix and 38 more in Game 2, but the Lakers needed Kobe's dramatic jump shot with 2.6 seconds left to win Game 2. Moving to Phoenix, Shaq was just as uncontrollable in Game 3, powering his way to 37 points. But the Lakers fell flat in Game 4, and the Suns burned them with their great guards, Jason Kidd and Penny Hardaway. Coming back home to STAPLES Center, the Lakers played their best defense of the playoffs in Game 5, smothering the Suns in an overpowering team effort.

GAME 1
LAKERS 105, Suns 77

GAME 2
LAKERS 97, Suns 96

GAME 3
SUNS 105, Lakers 99

GAME 4
SUNS 117, Lakers 98

GAME 5
LAKERS 87, Suns 65

29

Home team in CAPS

ANSWERING THE BIG CHALLENGE

All season long, Portland had been the Lakers' stiffest competition. The stage was set for a dramatic Western Conference Finals, and both teams rose to the occasion. Shaq was tremendous in Game 1 with 41 points, 11 rebounds and 7 assists, foiling Portland's "Hack-a-Shaq" plan by making some clutch free throws. But in Game 2, the Trail Blazers, led by Rasheed Wallace and Scottie Pippen, blew out the Lakers by 29 points.

With the pressure on in Portland, the Lakers came through with flying colors. Kobe, playing with a sprained right foot, dramatically saved Game 3 when he blocked Arvydas Sabonis's last-second shot, and Shaq made all nine of his free throws to spur a Game 4 triumph.

In control, 3-1, the Lakers let Game 5 slip away at home, and when Portland came back home to win Game 6, the season came down to Game 7, which turned out to be one of the greatest in NBA history. The Blazers jumped ahead by 16 points early in the fourth quarter, but Kobe blocked a shot by Bonzi Wells to start a 15-0 run that got the Lakers even. The most sensational play of the series—Kobe throwing a lob pass that Shaq dunked from two feet above the basket—rocked STAPLES Center and was the knockout punch in the most dramatic comeback victory in the team's history. The Lakers were Western Conference champions.

GAME 1
LAKERS 109, Portland 94

GAME 2
Portland 106, LAKERS 77

GAME 3
Lakers 93, PORTLAND 91

GAME 4
Lakers 103, PORTLAND 91

GAME 5
Portland 96, LAKERS 88

GAME 6
PORTLAND 103, Lakers 93

GAME 7
LAKERS 89, Portland 84

Home team in CAPS

NO HANDS PLEASE! KOBE BRYANT DISSUADES ARVYDAS SABONIS FROM TRYING TO STOP HIM FROM THROWING DOWN A BIG-TIME DUNK.

PLAYOFFS
NBA FINALS

CHAMPS AT LAST!

With the first championship of his life so close, Shaq breathed deeply and blew away the Indiana Pacers in one of the most dominating NBA Finals performances in league history.

Shaq scored 43 points with 19 rebounds in Game 1, then came back with 40 points and 24 rebounds in Game 2, while setting an all-time NBA record with 39 free-throw attempts, making 18. Glen Rice and Ron Harper picked up the slack with 21 points each after Kobe sprained his left ankle early in Game 2.

Down 2-0, the Pacers came alive at Conseco Fieldhouse, winning Game 3, thanks to the great shooting of Reggie Miller (33 points) and Jalen Rose (21 points). Shaq scored 33, but the Lakers missed Kobe badly.

In Game 4, Kobe came back and was brilliant in overtime, scoring eight of the Lakers' 16 overtime points and leading them to the 120-118 win. Game 5 was all Indiana, sending the series back to Los Angeles. With Shaq scoring 41 points, Kobe 26 and Rice 16, the Lakers held off the Pacers in Game 6, becoming champions at last—the first time since 1988. Welcome back, Lakers!

GAME 1
LAKERS 104, Pacers 87

GAME 2
LAKERS 111, Pacers 104

GAME 3
PACERS 100, Lakers 91

GAME 4
Lakers 120, PACERS 118 (OT)

GAME 5
PACERS 120, Lakers 87

GAME 6
LAKERS 116, Pacers 111

Home team in CAPS

THE INDIANA PACERS COULD ONLY WATCH IN AWE AS SHAQUILLE O'NEAL DROPS TWO EASY POINTS AGAINST THE EASTERN CONFERENCE CHAMPIONS.

ALL-TIME LEADERS

GAMES:

Kareem Abdul-Jabbar	1,093
Jerry West	932
James Worthy	926
Magic Johnson	906
Michael Cooper	873

TOTAL POINTS:

Jerry West	25,192
Kareem Abdul-Jabbar	24,176
Elgin Baylor	23,149
Magic Johnson	17,707
James Worthy	16,320

ASSISTS:

Magic Johnson	10,141
Jerry West	6,238
Norm Nixon	3,846
Michael Cooper	3,666
Kareem Abdul-Jabbar	3,652

REBOUNDS:

Elgin Baylor	11,463
Kareem Abdul-Jabbar	10,279
Magic Johnson	6,559
Wilt Chamberlain	6,524
Vern Mikkelsen	5,940

STEALS:

Magic Johnson	1,724
James Worthy	1,041
Byron Scott	1,038
Michael Cooper	1,033
Kareem Abdul-Jabbar	983

BLOCKED SHOTS:

Kareem Abdul-Jabbar	2,694
Elden Campbell	1,006
Vlade Divac	833
James Worthy	624
Elmore Smith	609

REGULAR SEASON RECORD HOLDERS

(Single Game)

POINTS:

71 Elgin Baylor (vs. New York, 11/15/60)

FIELD GOALS:

29 Wilt Chamberlain (vs. Phoenix, 2/9/69)

FREE THROWS:

22 Larry Foust (vs. St. Louis, 11/30/57)

REBOUNDS:

42 Wilt Chamberlain (vs. Boston, 3/7/69)

ASSISTS:

24 Magic Johnson (vs. Denver, 11/17/89; vs. Phoenix 1/9/90)

THREE-POINT FIELD GOALS:

8 Glen Rice (vs. Portland, 5/5/99); Nick Van Exel (vs. Dallas, 12/13/94; vs. Denver, 2/13/97; vs. Dallas, 3/4/97)

BLOCKED SHOTS:

17 Elmore Smith (vs. Portland, 10/28/73)

STEALS:

10 Jerry West (vs. Seattle, 12/7/73)

MINUTES:

64 Norm Nixon (vs. Cleveland, 1/29/80)

CONSECUTIVE FIELD GOALS:

14 Wilt Chamberlain (vs. Detroit, 3/11/69)